Choosing My First

Roger Banks, Barry Carpenter and Diviyha Ramalingham
illustrated by Lucy Bergonzi

Series Consultant: Kathy Melling

Beyond Words

London

36

First published in the UK 2018 by Books Beyond Words.

Text & illustrations © Books Beyond Words, 2018.

ISBN 978-1-78458-097-1

British Library Cataloguing-in-Publication Data

A catalogue record for this book is available from the British Library.

Printed by Lamport Gilbert Ltd, Reading.

Books Beyond Words is a Community Interest Company registered in England and Wales (7557861).

Further information about the Books Beyond Words series can be obtained from Beyond Words' website: www.booksbeyondwords.co.uk.

Contents

page

Choosing My First Job

Work is something that everyone should be encouraged to aim for when they leave school or college. For Zac, Chelsea and Amy it is just a matter of finding the job and route that fits them best. Zac's not sure that work is for him, and his teacher has to think creatively to help him try out a job that matches his interests perfectly. For Chelsea, a period of work experience and trying out different tasks helps to identify the right job. Amy does a college course and travel training alongside her work placement to get all the experience and qualifications she needs for the career she wants. *Choosing My First Job* will help young people understand that work is for everyone, that finding the right job feels brilliant and there are lots of different ways of getting there.

Reading Books Beyond Words to help think about work

This mini series of four books has been co-created with people with learning disabilities to help young people and adults think about work and to imagine themselves in work. These straightforward picture stories introduce practical information about choosing and getting a job, about settling in and doing a job, and about enjoying being in work.

The stories are based on issues that affect many people who we think will find the books' approach relevant and helpful, including young people with special educational needs and those with a range of impairments and health conditions.

You won't find every possible work situation or choice in these stories. Rather they can help the person or group you are supporting to reflect on their own hopes and experiences, even if they are quite different from what's in the story. This way you can start conversations about what people want to do themselves, or what work is like for them. Many readers like to name the people in the story. This can increase empathy with *all* the characters and help readers to think about even minor characters' stories and choices.

If you are reading this book in a community, school or college book club, you might consider inviting a work advisor to come and meet the group, to hear their ideas and answer any questions they have. This can also be an opportunity for individual members to arrange an appointment with the advisor to explore their own work aspirations further.

Why are there no words?

Many people find pictures much easier for following stories or learning new information than words, whether written or spoken. It's tempting to think that pictures are for children and are just a means to learn to read, but this isn't true. From the earliest times people have used pictures to pass on stories from generation to generation, or to give meaningful instructions where words are confusing; think about the way that pictures and diagrams are used in everyday situations to give instructions for cooking, crafts or building flat-pack furniture. Getting meaning from pictures is an essential skill, and one we learn early on.

Words, on the other hand, can create a barrier for people who find it hard to read, or they can put off people who had a difficult time at school with words and literacy. Combining words and pictures can also make understanding harder for some people, even if they are good readers.

How to read stories told in pictures

The most important thing to remember is that every reader will create a different version of the story. This is fine. There is no right or wrong story; what matters is the one that makes sense to the particular person or group exploring what work means to them. Your story – if you are a support worker, parent or job coach – is your own, and may be quite different from the one the reader sees.

Giving up control over the story can be difficult; staying quiet and letting the person explore the pictures is a skill that takes practice. Gentle prompts will usually give you a lot more information about the reader than supplying fixed answers.

Making it real

Individual readers will have different starting points. For example, some people start with the 'action' in the picture, noticing what people are doing or where they are, and often wanting to give names to all of the characters. This is useful to provide context. Other layers of reading include what characters are thinking, feeling or saying.

An important moment when reading together is to notice when to make the switch from the fiction of the narrative in the story to real-life situations. We can do this with a graded set of questions that move the focus of the conversation from what's happening in the story to what a reader's own ideas, hopes and aspirations might be.

We call this the 'exploratory' or 'predictive' level of reading, where we start to imagine or predict things that are not in the story but can be related to our own lives.

To support the switch from fiction to reality:

1. start with "who?" and "what?" questions: "Who is that?" "What is happening?" "What are they doing?"
2. move on to more open prompts such as "I wonder what it would be like to ... be a volunteer/be at work"

3. switch to making the link with the person's own experiences and thoughts, for example: "Would you like to ... volunteer/work?" "Has that happened to you?"

Extending the reading to practical activities

Here are some ideas for creative ways to build on the story created and to support and develop people's ideas about work.

Together on a big sheet of paper draw an outline of someone with a job/without a job – this could be a photo of the person themselves. Note what feelings and activities the person associates with work, any worries or hopes, or steps they might take to prepare for work.

Draw a 'Me Map' or spider diagram with a photo of the person in the middle and a title like: 'What will help me think about getting a job'/'What will help me think about volunteering'. List all the things that the person wants to learn or try out as part of their journey towards work. Some people might like to use pictures from magazines or the internet.

Take photos of people in a 'freeze frame', like a statue of a person in different situations: before going to work, getting ready in the morning, travelling to work, and at work. You could use pictures from these books as models. Use these freeze frames as key points along a timeline of a day at work, drawn on a long sheet of paper. The timeline could include different people you might meet along the way, what you might talk to them about, things you look forward to during the day, and what your job might be.

Supporting an individual or members of a group to start thinking about work

You can help each person to think about themselves as someone who could have a job and a career, and could make a valuable contribution to the workplace. Here are some group activities which can help to build people's confidence in their own transferable skills and personal qualities. In each case, you can give as much support with reading or writing or choosing a picture as each member needs.

Write each person's name at the top of a piece of paper or card. Pass the paper/card around the group for other people to add a word or picture showing what they like about the person, or something that person is good at. When everyone has added something to the list, each person reads out what is on their own paper/card, with help if needed, finding out how other people see them, and giving them the opportunity to think and talk about themselves in a positive way.

Building on the activity above, ask people to think about their interests, hobbies and other things they are good at. Help them use these ideas to make a collage with pictures of their preferred activities or a spider diagram using words or drawings if they prefer. Share each collage or spider diagram with the group, and think together about what jobs people can do that fit with their skills and interests.

The right to work and mental wellbeing

Everyone has the right to work. Our job and our career are often a big part of who we are and how we think about ourselves. Work also brings with it important benefits like money, social capital and wellbeing. People with learning disabilities have the same rights as everyone else, and the evidence shows that starting work with a supportive employer is the best way to support them to take up their right to work. This gives them the chance to take their place as active members of their communities and wider society, as well as bring a rich variety of skills and talents to the workplace.

It is known that being in work can have a positive effect on our wellbeing. As well as providing money and other things we need for daily life, it can bring self-esteem, companionship and status. Having a job gives:

- opportunities for social contacts and support

- structure to how we use our time

- physical and mental activity

- the chance to develop skills

- a sense of identity and personal achievement

- greatly increased confidence and a feeling of 'being like everyone else'.

These can also be important in helping the recovery of people who are mentally and/or physically unwell.

Finding the right employment support

Starting a job can be a confusing experience, and it's common to feel anxious, uncertain and tired. For many people with a learning disability, good employment support is critical to getting and keeping a job.

Supported employment, or job coaching, has for many years been a successful way of supporting people with learning disabilities to get and keep paid jobs. The model uses a partnership approach to help people find employment that lasts, and to help businesses employ valuable workers. Supported employment does not focus on getting people 'ready' for work through training or basic qualifications; it is about giving good quality, person-centred support to find the right job for the right person, then getting training and support in place to help them enjoy work and stay there. This is called place, train and maintain.

Finding good quality employment support can be difficult. If you aren't eligible for Local Authority support, this may affect your access to supported employment, and the people with the right expertise might be found in different places, depending on the area you live in. This can include schools, colleges, supported employment agencies, training providers and Jobcentre Plus.

If you need help finding a supported employment provider in your local area, or are finding it hard to get access to the level of support you need to get or stay in work, there are organisations that can help. The British Association of Supported Employment is the national trade association for the sector and maintains a list of local providers, as well as best practice standards and resources (see page 61).

It is important that support is provided by someone who is trained to the National Occupational Standards for Supported Employment Practitioners. Here are some questions you can ask to see if the support on offer from providers is good quality and evidence-based:

- How long have you been supporting people to find and keep jobs?

- Do you believe that everyone who wants to work, can work, with the right job and the right support?

- What types of jobs have you helped people to find? How many hours do they work and what is their rate of pay?

- How will you get to know me?

- How do you let employers know about what you do?

- How will you involve me in the process of finding a job?

- How will you present my skills and abilities to an employer?

- How will you support me to learn my job?

- What support will you give to the employer?

- How will you support me to keep my job and progress my career?

- Will you help me with my benefits to make sure that I am financially better off in work?

- Have you ever supported someone who has a disability similar to mine?

- Have you ever excluded people from using your services? Why?

- Do you have any recommendations from those who use your services, families or employers?

Starting to think about work

Preparing for adult life must start as early as possible to allow young people to develop the skills and knowledge to have choice and control. From Year 9 (age 14) onwards, the most recent special educational needs and disability (SEND) reforms in England and Wales require schools and other organisations to focus on ordinary life outcomes such as paid employment, independent living, community participation, and health and wellbeing. A joined-up approach is needed, that involves the young person fully, and takes into account all aspects of their life and the services they use. In fact, many schools are starting to talk to learners and their families about 'what you want to be' in the Early Years, encouraging them to plan and prepare a 'road map for life'.

People with learning difficulties and disabilities have always faced multiple barriers to employment, contributing to poorer life outcomes, but this is gradually changing. Schools and Local Authorities are working more closely with employers, helping to remove the barriers to career opportunities they might have experienced in the past. They are getting better at futures planning, for example using wikis and personal profiles to support young people in recognising their strengths and ambitions. Other new approaches, including this series of books, are helping to raise the aspirations of young people and their families. These initiatives allow them to communicate more effectively and widen their opportunities for work and employment.

Making transition work better

Young people's experiences of moving on from education vary widely. We are learning more about what works in supporting young people to have a positive experience of transition and to start out in adult life with good prospects. Barriers include a lack of good information, and a shortage of time to make plans. There is often a lack of continuity between professionals working with families as young people move from children's services to adults' services.

The main focus is on making transition work better, and supporting young people to have access to the things that make up fulfilling adult lives, such as:

- paid employment and higher education

- adult education

- independent living opportunities

- good health

- friends, relationships and being part of the community.

The Children and Families Act 2014 aimed to change how families, schools and employers think about the future of young people with learning difficulties and disabilities. At its heart was a commitment to ensuring that children, young people and their families are at the centre of decision-making about their health, education and social experiences. Under the Act, all Statements of Special Needs are transferring to Education Health and Care Plans, with the aim of fitting provision better to the needs of the individual child or young person. EHC Plans offer some decision-making rights and responsibilities for young people from 16 onwards, and can remain in place until the age of 25.

Features of the new approach are:

- a focus on better life outcomes in employment; independent living; community inclusion, friends and relationships; and good health

- more emphasis on the involvement of young people and their families

- better joint working by education, health and social care provision

- personal budgets as part of the EHC Plan

- encouraging young people to think about hopes and dreams, and to plan for a better future

- person-centred planning.

The underlying principles of person-centred practice are about improving people's life chances, and for this to work, the team of support around a young person needs to start early on.

The Local Offer can support young people and their families to make full use of resources that exist locally, including supported employment. The Local Offer is a Local Authority's publication, usually a website, designed to provide clear, comprehensive, accessible and up-to-date information. It also aims to make provision more responsive to local needs and aspirations by directly involving young people and their parents, and service providers, in developing and reviewing the Offer.

Moving forward into work

Supporting a young person to move from education into work can happen in any number of ways, and should work flexibly to take account of all their strengths, aspirations and interests.

Schools are starting to link more effectively with employers and there are many successful examples of partnerships establishing pathways into work and independent living.

Supported internships

A supported internship is a full-time study programme specially devised to help young people develop the skills they need to find and stay in paid employment through learning in the workplace. These programmes are aimed at young people in their final year of education who have a current Education Health and Care Plan, stating that they would benefit from this type of provision to help them find a job.

Internships last for a minimum of six months but, more usually, up to nine months. Most of the internship is spent in a work placement, where the young people learn alongside regular staff. The placements are unpaid and can be with any type of employer. Some programmes use a single employer within a service industry, such as a hotel or hospital or a Local Authority, as they can offer a wide variety of work opportunities and placement experiences. Others use a range of employers, including small- to medium-size businesses as well as larger employers, depending on the local job market and the young person's aspirations.

During the internship the young person and the employer will have the support of a job coach trained in supported employment, who will support the young person to learn the job step by step, if needed. Equally importantly, the job coach will support the employer both to understand the business case for employing a diverse workforce, and to get to grips with reasonable adjustments at work, to increase their disability confidence.

As well as their time with the employer, the young person will have an individual, classroom-based study programme. This will include functional English and Maths needed for the job, as well as any relevant qualifications, for example health and safety, food hygiene and so on, and other 'soft' skills, like communicating well, sorting out problems and working as part of a team.

At the end of the internship, if there is a vacancy that the young person is suited to, they can be offered paid employment within the company. Where this isn't possible, the job coach will support the young person to look for other employment as part of their study programme. In both cases the job coach will make sure the young person and employer have ongoing support through the 'place, train and maintain' supported employment model.

In England and Wales, supported internships are provided by schools, colleges and training providers, and can be in partnership with a supported employment service and an employer or employers, and funded by the Education and Skills Funding Agency. They should form part of each area's SEND Local Offer. There is no central register for supported internships and different providers and areas may follow different models, but individual examples of good practice can be found in government and voluntary sector guidance.

Useful resources in the UK

Mencap
www.mencap.org.uk
A national organisation aiming to improve the lives of people with learning disabilities and autism and their families. Mencap conducts research and campaigns and offers advice, resources and support, including a national Helpline. Via its network of local member organisations, Mencap provides direct services to people and their families, including social activities, learning and employment support.
Helpline: 0808 808 1111
helpline@mencap.org.uk

Jobcentre Plus
www.gov.uk/contact-jobcentre-plus
If you are over 18, your local Jobcentre can help you learn new skills and find a job, tell you about disability-friendly employers in your area and discuss other support that may be available to you. You may wish to make an appointment to see a disability employment advisor, who will be able to give you personalised advice. You find contact details for your nearest Jobcentre branch online.

Citizens Advice Bureau
www.citizensadvice.org.uk
Citizens Advice provides free, confidential and independent advice online, over the phone and in person in their local branches. Advisors can inform you about your rights and talk to you about any problems you are facing in the workplace and how

to solve them. You can search online to find contact details for your nearest branch.
Tel (England): 03444 111 444
Tel (Wales): 03444 77 20 20

British Association for Supported Employment (BASE)
www.base-uk.org
A membership organisation that exists to develop and encourage best practice in supported employment, through advising on policy development and providing information, training and consultancy. A list of their current member organisations who provide supported employment services can be found on their website. Each of these organisations is working in some way to support people with disabilities or other disadvantages into sustainable employment.
Tel: 01204 880733
admin@base-uk.org

The National Autistic Society (NAS)
www.autism.org.uk
A national charity providing information, support and specialist services as well as campaigning to improve the lives of people with autism (including Asperger syndrome) and their families. NAS has a network of support centres and enterprise activities that give people the opportunity to develop their skills, prepare for work and find a job they can do well and enjoy. NAS also offers information, advice and training for employers to guide them in how to recruit and best support autistic employees.
Helpline: 0808 800 4104
nas@nas.org.uk

ENABLE Scotland
www.enable.org.uk
A Scottish charity working to improve the lives of people with a learning disability and their families. Through the ENABLE Works service, adults and young people can access support to prepare for the workplace and find the job that's right for them. Employers can also get advice and support to help them recruit and retain staff with learning disabilities.
Tel: 0300 0200 101
enabledirect@enable.org.uk

Disability Law Service
www.dls.org.uk
A charity providing free legal information, advice and representation to people with disabilities and their families. If you feel that you have been discriminated against because of your disability you can contact the DLS for advice.
Tel: 0207 791 9800
advice@dls.org.uk

National Development Team for inclusion (NDTi)
www.ndti.org.uk
NDTi is a not-for-profit organisation that exists to ensure that people with disabilities and older people have choice and control over their own lives. They carry out policy development, consultancy, training, research and evaluation around different issues including employment.
Tel: 01225 789135
office@ndti.org.uk

Preparing for Adulthood programme
www.preparingforadulthood.org.uk
The Preparing for Adulthood programme (PfA) is run by NDTi and aims to ensure Local Authorities and other organisations are supported and equipped to successfully help young people into adulthood with paid employment, good health, independent living and friends, relationships and community inclusion. Resources for professionals are freely available to download from their website on topics including supported internships and employment.
Tel: 01225 789135
info@preparingforadulthood.org.uk

Transition Information Network (TIN)
Overseen by the Council for Disabled Children, TIN is a hub of information for young people with disabilities, their families and professionals who work with them, including a dedicated section for sources of information and support relating to employment.
www.councilfordisabledchildren.org.uk/transition-information-network

When I Grow Up: facilitator's handbook
A handbook produced by the Foundation for People with Learning Disabilities to help schools raise the aspirations of pupils with learning disabilities around work and employment. The handbook includes session plans for 10 classroom workshops and some family workshops.
www.mentalhealth.org.uk/learning-disabilities/publications/when-i-grow-up-wigu-handbook-teachers

Related titles in the Books Beyond Words series

Rose Gets in Shape (2016) by Roger Banks and Paul Wallang, illustrated by Mike Nicholson. Rose lives on her own and she has picked up some bad habits about eating and taking exercise. Her energy is low and she gets tired easily. When her doctor tells her that her weight is causing health problems she decides to get in shape. We follow Rose through the struggles and triumphs of her weight loss journey, the new activities she takes up, and the good friends and support she finds along the way.

George Gets Smart (2001) by Sheila Hollins, Margaret Flynn and Philippa Russell, illustrated by Catherine Brighton. George's life changes when he learns how to keep clean and smart. People no longer avoid being with him and he enjoys the company of his workmates and friends.

Belonging (2018) Sheila Hollins, Valerie Sinason and Access All Areas artists, illustrated by Lucy Bergonzi. Kali is lonely. She has no real friends and no reason to leave the house to socialise; community activities seem remote and pointless to her. Outside her home, Kali defends herself with a mask of hostility, hiding her true feelings. But when things go wrong, Kali finds herself in a position to help Stefan, another vulnerable and lonely person. In the aftermath, they forge a friendship and begin to find themselves in the centre of a community where they feel they belong.

Michelle Finds a Voice (2016, 2nd edition) by Sheila Hollins and Sarah Barnett, illustrated by Denise Redmond. Michelle cannot speak and is unable to communicate her thoughts and feelings. She feels isolated and unhappy. Michelle and her carers try signing, symbols and electronic aids to find a solution that works.

Speaking Up for Myself (reissued 2017) by Sheila Hollins, Jackie Downer, Linnett Farquarson and Oyepeju Raji, illustrated by Lisa Kopper. Having a learning disability and being from an ethnic minority group can make it hard to get good services. Natalie learns to fix problems by being assertive and getting help from someone she trusts.

Authors and artist

Roger Banks is a Psychiatrist for people with learning disabilities and a Director of Beyond Words. He is a Fellow and former Vice-President of the Royal College of Psychiatrists, an Honorary Fellow of the Royal College of General Practitioners and a Fellow of the Institute of Psychotherapy and Disability. He is President of the European Association for Mental Health and Disability and is currently the Senior Psychiatry Lead in the Learning Disability Programme of NHS England.

Professor Barry Carpenter CBE is Honorary Professor at the Universities of Worcester, Limerick, Hamburg and Flinders, and Professor of Mental Health in Education at Oxford Brookes University. Barry has been Headteacher, Inspector of Schools and Director of the Centre for Special Education at Westminster College, Oxford. In 2009, he was appointed by the Secretary of State for Education as Director of the Children with Complex Learning Difficulties and Disabilities Research Project.

Diviyha Ramalingham attended Cricket Green School in Mitcham where she completed work placements at local nurseries and used her experiences to help co-author this book. She is now at college and is enjoying spending time with new people she has met there. Diviyha is hoping her next move will be on a supported internship.

Lucy Bergonzi has worked as a muralist, theatre designer and community artist. For many years she worked in the voluntary and community sector, with wide experience of supporting people with learning disabilities. She is the illustrator of *A Day at the Beach*, *Going to Church* and *Belonging* for Books Beyond Words. Lucy's website is www.lucybergonzi. co.uk.

Kathy Melling has worked in the supported employment sector since the late 1970s, first in the US, studying under Marc Gold, the founder of Training in Systematic Instruction and supported employment at the University of Illinois. She emigrated to the UK in the early 1980s and her pioneering work in Kent, transforming day services and developing supported employment, featured in the King's Fund 'Changing Days' research project. She became the National Employment Lead for Valuing People Now in 2009, and helped establish the British Association of Supported Employment, where she is still an active member of the National Executive Committee. She now works as an independent trainer and consultant, working on the introduction of National Occupational Standards and leading on employment and supported internships for the Preparing for Adulthood programme.

Acknowledgments

We are grateful to Margaret Mulholland and Swiss Cottage School for additional text in this book, and for the advice and support of our advisory group: Mel Kew, Callum Thornton, Antoinette Cole, Quilenn Huntesmith, John Byrne, Francesca Cappelli, Beth Madigan, Kirsten Lawrence, Etherline Joseph, Suzanne Thomson, Rosie Harland, Sue North, Jackie Scarrott, Kevin Preen, Paul Hayton and Mina Scarlett.

Many thanks to all individuals and groups who trialled the pictures, including Lambeth College Preparation to Work class in connection with The Camden Society as part of the Lambeth Prowork Project July 2017; Dynamite Portsmouth: Olivia Parry, Carly Blake; The Beacon School, Folkestone; Cricket Green School, supported by Mel: Sophie, Riana, Tobi and Nathan; Carwarden House Sixth Form students; Hamilton Lodge School and College, Brighton; Pluss, part of Plymouth People First: Zoe, Tina, Roberto, Max, Debbie, Chaz, Gary and Lizzie, supported by Jill Singh; Hannah O'Dwyer, Bernie O'Dwyer; Volunteering Matters: John, Carly and Richard; Xena Tique; Volunteering Matters Futures Project: Oliver, Alexandra, William; Lexden Springs School; Queensmill School; Lambeth College; Bromley Mencap; Whitehorse hub at Croydon Central Library: Tina, Maybelle, Ian, David, Jacqui, Sandra, Lloyd, Sarah; Orchard Hill College/Speak Up Sutton: Ifeoma, Rees, Robert, Moshin, Todd, Armani; Olympus L.I.V.E: Vivien, Anita, Philip, Antony.

Our illustrator Lucy is grateful to Warwickshire College's Supported Learning Department, to 'Dr Um' drum shop in Leamington Spa, and to Age UK Coventry's woodwork centre. And to her models Amy K., Amy S., Becky, Carol, Ellen, Emel, James, Lily, Mattie, Ola, Olivia, Richard, Rosie, Sasha, Steve and Vic for their help when she was creating the pictures for *Choosing My First Job*.

Finally we are grateful to the Department for Work and Pensions for their generous financial support of this book and wider project.

Beyond Words: publications and training

Books Beyond Words are stories for anyone who finds pictures easier than words. A list of all Beyond Words publications, including print and eBook versions of Books Beyond Words titles, and where to buy them, can be found on our website:

www.booksbeyondwords.co.uk

Workshops for family carers, support workers and professionals about using Books Beyond Words are provided regularly in London, or can be arranged on request in other localities or to cover specific areas of interest. Self-advocates are welcome. For information about forthcoming training, please contact us:

email: admin@booksbeyondwords.co.uk

Video clips showing our books being read are also on our website and YouTube channel: www.youtube.com/user/booksbeyondwords and on our DVD, *How to Use Books Beyond Words*.

How to read this book

This is a story for people who find pictures easier to understand than words. It is not necessary to be able to read any words at all.

1. Some people are not used to reading books. Start at the beginning and read the story in each picture. Encourage the reader to hold the book themselves and to turn the pages at their own pace.

2. Whether you are reading the book with one person or with a group, encourage them to tell the story in their own words. You will discover what each person thinks is happening, what they already know, and how they feel. You may think something different is happening in the pictures yourself, but that doesn't matter. Wait to see if their ideas change as the story develops. Don't challenge the reader(s) or suggest their ideas are wrong.

3. Some pictures may be more difficult to understand. It can help to prompt the people you are supporting, for example:

- I wonder who that is?
- I wonder what is happening?
- What is he or she doing now?
- I wonder how he or she is feeling?
- Do you feel like that? Has it happened to you/ your friend/ your family?

4. You don't have to read the whole book in one sitting. Allow people enough time to follow the pictures at their own pace.

5. Some people will not be able to follow the story, but they may be able to understand some of the pictures. Stay a little longer with the pictures that interest them.